GAME DAY: FOOTBALL

# RUNNING BACKS

By K.C. Kelley

Reading consultant: Cecilia Minden-Cupp, Ph.D.,
Literacy Specialist

**Gareth Stevens**
Publishing

Please visit our web site at www.garethstevens.com.
For a free catalog describing Gareth Stevens Publishing's list of high-quality books, call 1-800-542-2595 (USA)
or 1-800-387-3178 (Canada). Gareth Stevens Publishing's fax: 1-877-542-2596

Library of Congress Cataloging-in-Publication Data
Kelley, K. C.
        Running backs / by K.C. Kelley.
            p. cm. — (Game day. Football)
            Includes bibliographical references and index.
        ISBN-10: 1-4339-1963-X — ISBN-13: 978-1-4339-1963-3 (lib. bdg.)
        1. Running backs (Football)—United States—Juvenile literature.
        2. Running backs (Football)—United States—Biography—Juvenile literature.  I. Title.
    GV954.K45   2010
    796.332'24—dc22                                            2009002277

This edition first published in 2010 by
**Gareth Stevens Publishing**
A Weekly Reader® Company
1 Reader's Digest Road
Pleasantville, NY 10570-7000 USA

Copyright © 2010 by Gareth Stevens, Inc.

Executive Managing Editor: Lisa M. Herrington
Senior Editor: Brian Fitzgerald
Senior Designer: Keith Plechaty

Produced by Q2AMedia
Art Direction: Rahul Dhiman
Senior Designer: Dibakar Acharjee
Image Researcher: Kamal Kumar

**Photo credits**
Key: t = top, b = bottom, c = center, l = left, r = right
**Cover and title page:** Tom Dahlin/Getty Images.
Donald Miralle/Getty Images: 4, 5; Bettmann/Corbis: 6; Underwood & Underwood/Corbis: 7; Frank Rippon/NFL/
Getty Images: 8; David Drapkin/Getty Images: 9; Getty Images: 10; New York Times Co./Getty Images: 11; Focus
on Sport/Getty Images: 12; George Rose/Getty Images: 13; Ronald Martinez/Getty Images: 14; Glenn James/
NFL: 15; Scott Boehm/Getty Images: 16; Kevin Terrell/Getty Images: 17; Greg Trott/Getty Images: 18; Drew
Hallowell/Getty Images: 19; Paul Jasienski/Getty Images: 20; Paul Spinelli/Getty Images: 21; Al Pereira/Getty
Images: 22; Michael Fabus/Getty Images: 23; Paul Spinelli/Getty Images: 24–25; Dilip Vishwanat/Getty Images:
26; Michael Zagaris/Getty Images: 27; Al Bello/Getty Images: 28; Kevin Terrell/Getty Images: 29; Paul Jasienski/
Getty Images: 30; Greg Trott/Getty Images: 31; Paul Spinelli/Getty Images: 32; Greg Trott/Getty Images: 33;
Stephen Dunn/Getty Images: 34; Kevin Terrell/Getty Images: 35; Tom Hauck/Getty Images: 36; Kevin C. Cox/
Getty Images: 37; Greg Trott/Getty Images: 38; Drew Hallowell/Getty Images: 39; Mike Eliason: 40, 41, 42, 43;
Ron Vesely/Getty Images: 44; Doug Pensinger/Getty Images: 45.
Q2AMedia Art Bank: 16, 33.

Printed in the United States of America

1 2 3 4 5 6 7 8 9 14 13 12 11 10 09

**Cover:** Adrian Peterson of the Minnesota Vikings is one of the top running backs in pro football.

# Contents

Words in the glossary appear in **bold** type the first time they are used in the text.

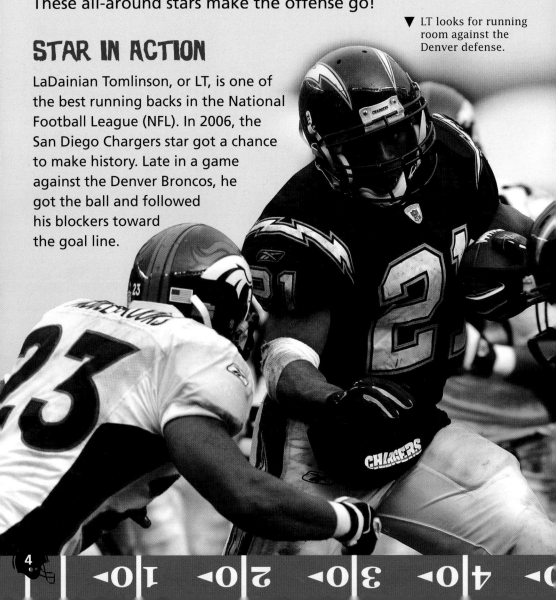

# Going for the Goal Line

Every NFL team needs good running backs.
These all-around stars make the offense go!

▼ LT looks for running room against the Denver defense.

## STAR IN ACTION

LaDainian Tomlinson, or LT, is one of the best running backs in the National Football League (NFL). In 2006, the San Diego Chargers star got a chance to make history. Late in a game against the Denver Broncos, he got the ball and followed his blockers toward the goal line.

# RECORD BREAKER

LT found a **hole** and burst into the end zone. Touchdown! It was his 28th touchdown of the season. The Chargers got the ball back soon after. This time, LT used his great speed to sprint downfield. Another touchdown! That gave him a total of 29 for the season—a new NFL record. LT is one of the best running backs in the league. Read on to find out more about the players who are always on the run!

## Name Game

The position of running back has had many names. They include tailback, halfback, fullback, scatback, and H-back. All those names mean slightly different things. But they all refer to players who run with the ball.

▶ Teammates congratulate LT after his record-setting touchdown.

### GLOSSARY

**hole:** an open area created by blockers into which a ball carrier can run

CHAPTER
1

# Birth of the Running Back

Football started in the 1880s. The forward pass, however, wasn't allowed until 1906. Teams could gain yards only by running the ball.

## ONE BIG PILE

Early football games were pretty boring. Offenses were not very creative. Blockers and defenders smashed together on almost every play. Runners usually ran a few yards and were slammed down. Everyone then got up and did it again.

▼ An early football team forms the flying wedge.

▲ The earliest football players didn't wear helmets. By the 1930s, most players wore leather helmets that offered some protection but had no facemasks.

## The Flying Wedge

One play in early football caused many problems. In the "flying wedge," a team formed a V, or wedge, with blockers. The blockers linked arms to shield the runner. The runner then got behind the wedge, and they all ran down the field. It was a dangerous play. Many defenders were injured trying to "break" the wedge. The play was soon **banned**.

## DANGER BALL

Years ago, football was more dangerous than it is today. Many plays ended with players in a big pile. Players didn't wear much padding. Many players were injured. Some were even killed. New rules and better equipment made the game safer—and more enjoyable for fans.

### GLOSSARY

**banned:** made illegal

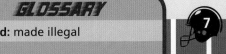

# SPEED AND POWER

Passing became popular in the 1940s. Defenders had to drop back off the **line of scrimmage** to cover receivers. That gave running backs more room to run. Runners started to gain more yards and score more touchdowns. By the 1950s, some runners were gaining 1,000 or more yards in a season.

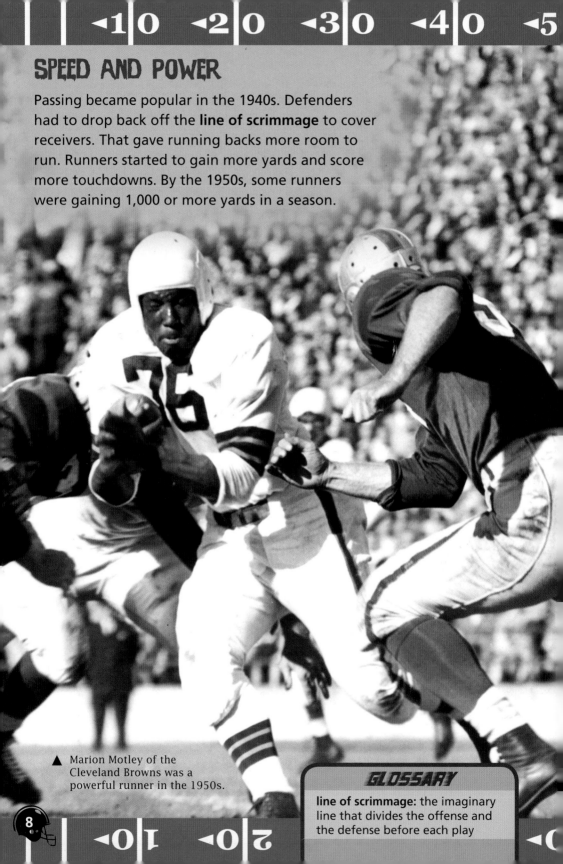

▲ Marion Motley of the Cleveland Browns was a powerful runner in the 1950s.

## GLOSSARY

**line of scrimmage:** the imaginary line that divides the offense and the defense before each play

# MANY SKILLS

The running back position continued to become more demanding. Today, running backs have to do it all. A top runner needs the strength to carry the ball for short gains. He needs speed to make long runs. He needs great hands for catching passes. He also needs skills to be a good blocker.

▲ Running backs do a lot more than run! Willie Parker of the Pittsburgh Steelers shows his skills as a pass catcher.

CHAPTER
2

# All-Time Greats

The running backs of today follow more than 75 years of great runners. Let's meet some of the top running backs in NFL history.

## THE GALLOPING GHOST

Red Grange was the first superstar running back. He gained fame in college at the University of Illinois. There, Grange got the nickname "the Galloping Ghost." Grange was speedy and powerful. In 1925, he joined the Chicago Bears. Huge crowds of fans turned out to see his games. Pro football might not have succeeded without Grange.

Footballs in Grange's time were larger and rounder than they are today.

## 40-Point Man

In a game in 1929, Ernie Nevers of the Chicago Cardinals set an NFL record that will probably live forever. He ran for six touchdowns for 36 points. He also kicked four **extra points**. His single-game total of 40 points is still an all-time record.

## BUSTIN' BRONKO

Bronko Nagurski was bigger than most players of the 1930s. The bruising runner was almost impossible to tackle. It usually took several defenders to bring him down. Even Nagurski's name sounded tough! He helped the Bears win NFL championships in 1932 and 1933.

### GLOSSARY

**extra points:** kicks, worth one point, that are attempted after a touchdown is scored

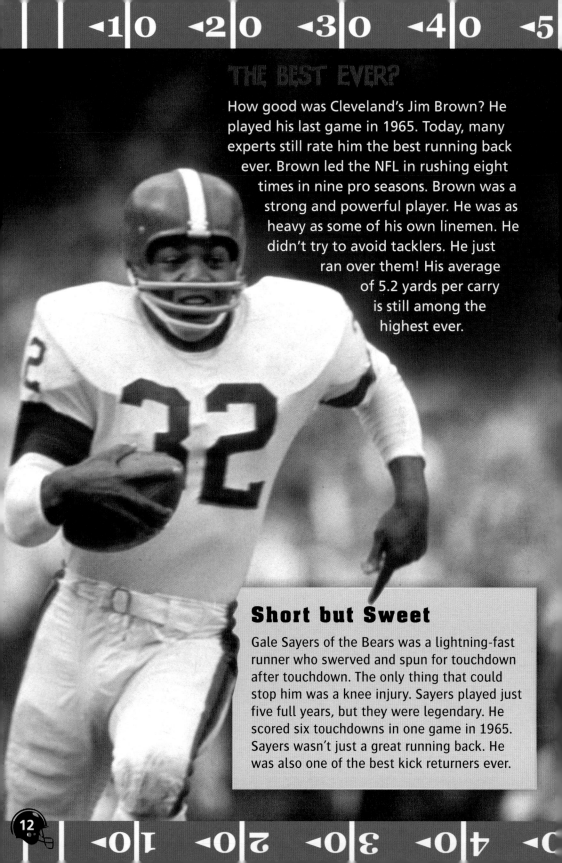

## THE BEST EVER?

How good was Cleveland's Jim Brown? He played his last game in 1965. Today, many experts still rate him the best running back ever. Brown led the NFL in rushing eight times in nine pro seasons. Brown was a strong and powerful player. He was as heavy as some of his own linemen. He didn't try to avoid tacklers. He just ran over them! His average of 5.2 yards per carry is still among the highest ever.

## Short but Sweet

Gale Sayers of the Bears was a lightning-fast runner who swerved and spun for touchdown after touchdown. The only thing that could stop him was a knee injury. Sayers played just five full years, but they were legendary. He scored six touchdowns in one game in 1965. Sayers wasn't just a great running back. He was also one of the best kick returners ever.

Some runners wear gloves for better grip on the football.

## SWEETNESS

Bears running back Walter Payton would take the ball—and then take off! Payton high-stepped, jumped, leaped, and powered his way to 16,726 yards. That's the second-highest rushing total of all time. He also helped Chicago win Super Bowl XX in 1986. Though he was a tough runner, Payton got his nickname "Sweetness" because of his pleasant personality.

# RECORD HOLDER

Emmitt Smith won just about every NFL award in his 15-year career. He was an NFL Most Valuable Player (MVP), a Super Bowl MVP, and an eight-time **Pro Bowl** player. Smith helped the Dallas Cowboys win three Super Bowls. He also led the NFL in rushing four times. His 18,355 rushing yards and 164 rushing touchdowns are the most of all time. Smith's toughness and ability to break tackles made him a legend.

▼ Emmitt Smith looks downfield as he outruns the defense.

# AMAZING MOVES

If defenders blinked, they might have missed Barry Sanders. The great Detroit Lions runner could turn a loss into a big gain with a twitch of his hips. He led the NFL in rushing four times. He also produced more amazing highlights than any other player in history. Sanders was the best runner in the NFL when he walked away from football after the 1998 season.

## A Special Club

Barry Sanders is one of only five players to run for more than 2,000 yards in a season. Eric Dickerson of the Los Angeles Rams set the all-time record when he gained an amazing 2,105 yards in 1984.

## GLOSSARY

**Pro Bowl:** the NFL's annual all-star game

**CHAPTER**

**3**

# Running Back Basics

Now that you've met the stars, let's find out how they do their jobs.

## WHERE TO START

Running backs begin most plays standing behind the quarterback. Two popular run **formations** in the NFL are the "I" and the "Pro Set." In the I, two running backs line up directly behind the quarterback. In the Pro Set, they stand behind and to the side. However, NFL teams use dozens of formations. Running backs can line up in many ways.

▼ The New York Giants use a version of the I formation. The fullback is not directly behind the quarterback.

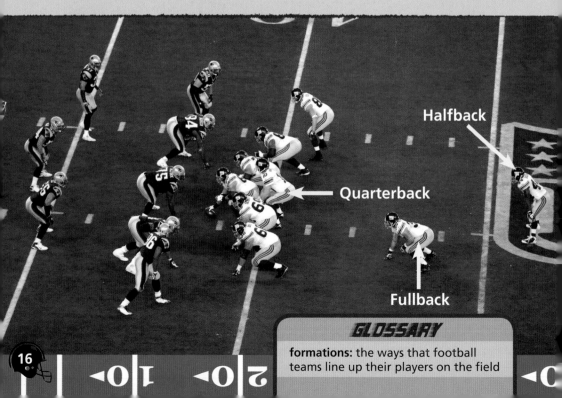

Halfback

Quarterback

Fullback

**GLOSSARY**

**formations:** the ways that football teams line up their players on the field

## HOW TO STAND

Before the snap, a running back often lines up in a two-point stance. He has two "points" on the ground—his feet! In a three-point stance, he leans forward with one hand resting on the ground. The three points are his two feet and one hand.

## Full or Half?

Many formations include two running backs. The fullback usually stands in front of a running back, or halfback. Fullbacks mostly block. They create holes for other runners. Fullbacks may also carry the ball. Fullbacks are usually bigger and stronger than halfbacks, but they aren't as fast.

▶ Carolina Panthers running back Jonathan Stewart (28) lines up in a two-point stance. In front of him, fullback Brad Hoover (45) takes a three-point stance.

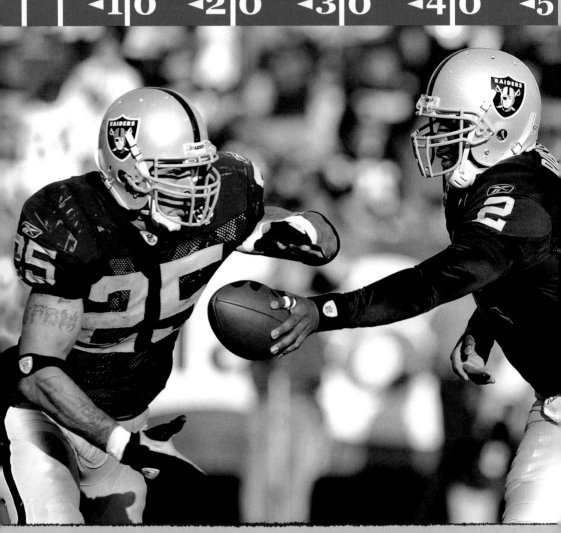

▲ Running back Justin Fargas of the Oakland Raiders gets ready to take a handoff from quarterback JaMarcus Russell.

# HANDOFFS

The basic way that the running back gets the ball is the handoff. The quarterback takes the snap from the center. Then he turns and holds out the ball to the side. The runner charges forward. Runners hold one hand above the other to receive the ball. The quarterback stuffs the ball into the runner's gut. The runner clamps his arms around the ball and heads toward the line of scrimmage.

# HERE'S THE PITCH

Some plays call for a back to run to the outside. That means he runs wide toward the sideline before turning to run upfield. On runs to the outside, the quarterback may **pitch**, or toss, the ball to the running back. After the snap, the quarterback turns and tosses the ball. The runner catches it while he's moving. Runners keep their eyes on the ball first and then look upfield once they catch it.

▼ Eli Manning of the Giants pitches the ball to running back Brandon Jacobs.

**GLOSSARY**

**pitch:** a soft, underhand toss backward

# Hold the Ball!

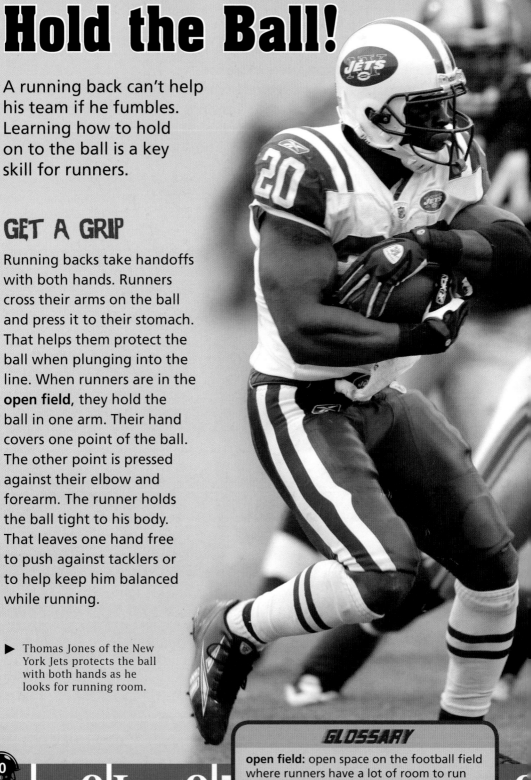

A running back can't help his team if he fumbles. Learning how to hold on to the ball is a key skill for runners.

## GET A GRIP

Running backs take handoffs with both hands. Runners cross their arms on the ball and press it to their stomach. That helps them protect the ball when plunging into the line. When runners are in the **open field**, they hold the ball in one arm. Their hand covers one point of the ball. The other point is pressed against their elbow and forearm. The runner holds the ball tight to his body. That leaves one hand free to push against tacklers or to help keep him balanced while running.

► Thomas Jones of the New York Jets protects the ball with both hands as he looks for running room.

### GLOSSARY

**open field:** open space on the football field where runners have a lot of room to run

## Protect the Rock!

Football players often call the football "the rock." Defenders try to "strip" the ball from runners by pulling on it. Runners practice proper technique so that they "protect the rock."

## CHANGING HANDS

Sometimes, a running back switches the ball from one hand to the other. When possible, he keeps it on the side away from the defense. He switches hands only when there's no danger of having the ball knocked loose. When being tackled, though, he should cover the ball with both hands.

► While running away from tacklers on his right, LaDainian Tomlinson carries the ball in his left hand.

Runners cover one point of the ball with their hand. They press the other point tight against their forearm.

# Time to Run!

Okay, the running back has the ball and he's holding on tightly. His next goal is to gain some yards!

## KNEES UP!

Running backs are coached to run with their knees high. That is especially important when running into the line. Why? A back who runs with his knees high is harder to tackle. He keeps going forward even if a defender hits them. He may also step over blockers or tacklers who are lying on the ground. Running backs develop big thigh muscles. Powerful legs are the "engine" that gives runners their speed.

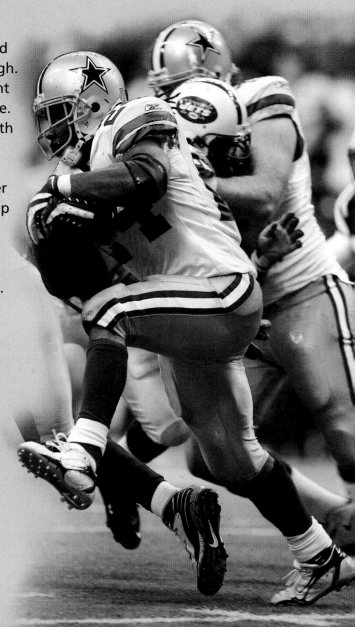

► Marion Barber of the Dallas Cowboys keeps his knees high as he hits the line of scrimmage.

▲ Jamal Lewis of the Cleveland Browns stays on his toes and keeps his shoulders square.

# MOVE THOSE FEET!

A running backs always keeps his feet moving. Even when he is being tackled, a running back keeps charging forward. That lets him break tackles and gain more yards. If he is grabbed around the chest, a runner keeps churning his feet. Often, he can shake free from a defender and pick up extra yards.

## Keep It Square

Running backs are taught to run with their chest pointing down the field. This keeps their shoulders "square." Running this way keeps a runner's body going forward, even as he is tackled.

# Follow Your Blockers

Without blockers, a running back has almost no chance. Running backs are taught to follow their blockers. If the blockers do their job, the runner just keeps going.

## HIT THE HOLE!

In football, a hole is the space between two blockers. Running backs train to run through holes. Each hole has a number. The number lets runners know how their teammates will block.

## Know Your Job

Before every play, the quarterback calls a play in the **huddle**. Each play has a code that tells blockers where to block and runners where to run. At the snap, each player must do his job properly for the play to succeed. Learning every play and paying attention in the huddle is important.

▼ LenDale White of the Tennessee Titans bursts through a hole created by his blockers.

## RUN TO DAYLIGHT

A hole might be open for only a split-second. Rushers are trained to run where they can see past the defense. Runners need great speed to burst through the holes like rockets. Of course, sometimes defenders break through the blockers. The hole closes up. Great running backs try to make their own holes.

### GLOSSARY

**huddle:** the gathering of a team's players before each play

# Popular Plays

Every team uses dozens of running plays. Certain plays, however, are common. Here's a look at three popular running plays in the NFL.

## OFF-TACKLE

Offensive tackles are some of the best—and biggest—blockers on a team. Off-tackle plays are run to the side of the line that includes a tackle and a tight end. That's called the strong side. The tackle makes a hole by blocking a defender toward the middle of the field. The running back rushes into that hole "off" the tackle, or he can rush farther outside "off" the tight end.

▶ Brandon Jacobs of the Giants runs through a hole created by tackle Kareem McKenzie (67).

# SWEEP

On some outside runs, the back follows a wall of blockers. A guard "pulls" out of the line at the snap. He runs to one side of the line and then upfield. The runner follows the guard as he "sweeps" up the field. The guard and other blockers clear the way. This gives the runner room to move. Once past the line, a runner might get a block from a wide receiver or a tight end.

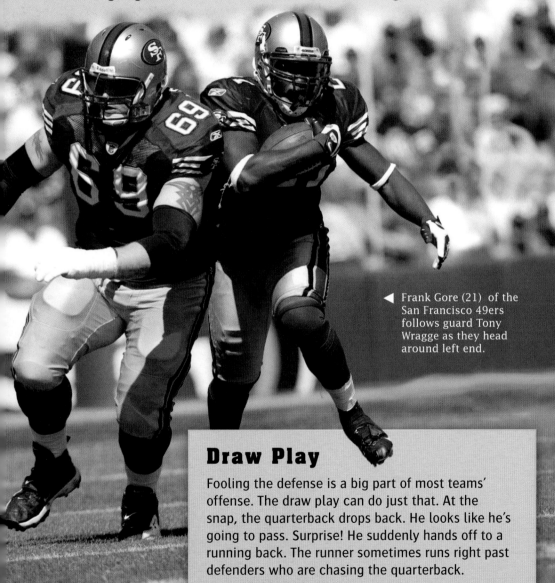

◀ Frank Gore (21) of the San Francisco 49ers follows guard Tony Wragge as they head around left end.

## Draw Play

Fooling the defense is a big part of most teams' offense. The draw play can do just that. At the snap, the quarterback drops back. He looks like he's going to pass. Surprise! He suddenly hands off to a running back. The runner sometimes runs right past defenders who are chasing the quarterback.

# Room to Run

Most running plays gain only a few yards. Sometimes, though, a running back bursts past the defensive linemen and linebackers. Then the race is on!

## SPEED PAYS OFF!

If a running back gets past the linebackers, only a **defensive back** (DB) can stop him. DBs are often the fastest players on a defense. The runner tries to find open space on the field. The defenders try to cut him off to make the tackle. This is when the runner's speed comes into play. Sometimes, a fast runner can simply run past tacklers.

▶ Brian Westbrook of the Philadelphia Eagles sprints away from Antonio Pierce of the New York Giants.

# MAKING THE MOVES

Runners use different moves to get away from tacklers. Tricky runners fake to one side or the other. They lean their head and shoulders one way and then turn quickly in another direction. They might run one way and then cut back in another direction. If the defender goes for the fake, then—zip!—the rusher speeds right by him.

Running backs may "stiff-arm" a tackler, or push him away with one hand. They may also spin, leap, or turn to avoid open-field tackles.

▶ Steven Jackson of the St. Louis Rams leaps over an Arizona Cardinals defender.

## GLOSSARY

**defensive back:** a defensive player who is usually assigned to cover a receiver

# Be a Receiver

Running backs don't just run, of course. They also catch passes. More and more, NFL teams use their running backs in the passing game.

Slaton is starting to look upfield to see where he has room to run. He has to make sure to secure the football first, though.

## HOW TO CATCH

Receivers catch the ball in a "basket." The position of a receiver's hands depends on where the ball is thrown. If the ball is at or above the chest, both of a receiver's thumbs and index fingers should be touching. If the pass is below the chest area, the pinky fingers should be touching to create a different basket area.

▶ Steve Slaton of the Houston Texans shows good pass-catching form on a screen pass.

## THE SCREEN PASS

One popular passing play for running backs is the screen pass. At the snap, the running back sprints to one side. As he does, several linemen move in front of him. The quarterback then passes the ball to the running back. He catches it and starts running behind the "screen" of linemen.

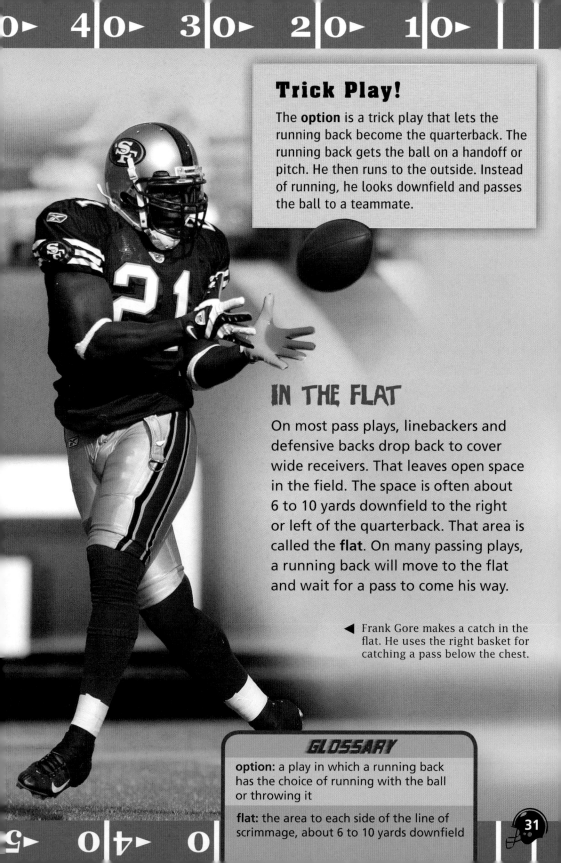

## Trick Play!

The **option** is a trick play that lets the running back become the quarterback. The running back gets the ball on a handoff or pitch. He then runs to the outside. Instead of running, he looks downfield and passes the ball to a teammate.

## IN THE FLAT

On most pass plays, linebackers and defensive backs drop back to cover wide receivers. That leaves open space in the field. The space is often about 6 to 10 yards downfield to the right or left of the quarterback. That area is called the **flat**. On many passing plays, a running back will move to the flat and wait for a pass to come his way.

◄ Frank Gore makes a catch in the flat. He uses the right basket for catching a pass below the chest.

### GLOSSARY

**option:** a play in which a running back has the choice of running with the ball or throwing it

**flat:** the area to each side of the line of scrimmage, about 6 to 10 yards downfield

# Be a Blocker

A running back has work to do even when he is not carrying or catching the ball. He helps his teammates by blocking on passing and running plays.

## PROTECT THE PASSER

Running backs protect the quarterback on some passing plays. Running backs stay in the backfield and block opposing rushers. Running backs might have to block big linebackers or speedy defensive ends.

▼ Running back Ray Rice (27) of the Baltimore Ravens makes a block to protect quarterback Joe Flacco (5).

▲ Fullback Mike Sellers (45) of the Washington Redskins clears a path for teammate Clinton Ports.

# HELP ANOTHER RUNNER

A running back might block for a fellow runner. A fullback often acts as the "lead blocker." Running backs might also block when the ball is handed off to a receiver on a **reverse**. On a reverse, a wide receiver takes a handoff as he runs from one side of the field to the other.

## Team Players

Fullbacks usually don't get much attention. Most fullbacks don't rack up a lot of yards or score many touchdowns. But they are key to a team's running game. Fullbacks make the blocks that often enable other players to reach the end zone.

## GLOSSARY

**reverse:** a running play that starts in one direction but quickly changes to the opposite direction. It often involves a running back handing off to a receiver.

# Stars of Today

Fast, strong, smart, and talented. Today's best running backs are some of the finest athletes in the NFL.

## STAR CHARGER

LaDainian "LT" Tomlinson might just become the best running back of all time. His record-setting 2006 season (see pages 4–5) was just one of many great years he has had with San Diego. Since joining the Chargers in 2001, LT has run for at least 1,100 yards and 10 touchdowns every season. Tomlinson is not just a great runner, however. He has caught more than 50 passes in each season of his career. He has also thrown for seven touchdowns! How does he do it? Speed, smarts, determination—they all add up to "superstar."

◄ LaDainian Tomlinson wears a plastic face shield with his facemask. This keeps tacklers' hands and fingers out of his face.

# FAST START

Adrian Peterson is the best young runner in the NFL. In his **rookie** season, he quickly became one of the league's top running backs. He started only nine games for the Minnesota Vikings, but he gained 1,341 yards. The highlight was when he gained 296 yards—in one game! That was the highest single-game total of all time. Peterson led the NFL in rushing in 2008 with 1,760 yards.

## GLOSSARY

**rookie:** a player in his first season of pro football

# WASHINGTON WINNER

It's one thing to be a big star for an NFL team. It's another to star for two teams! Clinton Portis ran for more than 1,500 yards in his first two seasons. He played for the Denver Broncos then. But Denver traded him to the Redskins in 2004. That was no problem for Portis, who gained at least 1,200 yards in four of his first five seasons with Washington. Portis combines power running with downfield speed.

▼ Clinton Portis shows off his moves and speed as he runs through a hole.

▲ Marion Barber shows off another running back skill: diving over a pile of players into the end zone.

# THE BARBER IS IN

After backing up Julius Jones for two years, Marion Barber took over as the Dallas Cowboys number-one back in 2007. He's a powerful runner who is great at fighting off tacklers. He has had at least 10 touchdowns in three seasons. Barber is a key part of Dallas's high-powered offense.

## Two in One

Some teams are blessed with two star running backs. Coaches can change them back and forth to keep both players rested. For example, in 2008, the New York Giants had two rushers top 1,000 yards: Brandon Jacobs and Derrick Ward. Jacobs is a power runner while Ward aims for speed. On the Carolina Panthers, DeAngelo Williams had 18 touchdowns in 2008. His running partner Jonathan Stewart scored 10 more!

# A NEW TURNER FOR ATLANTA

Michael Turner learned from the best. For four years, he was the number-one backup to LaDainian Tomlinson in San Diego. When Turner did get in, he played well. But he wanted a chance to be a starter. In 2008, Turner signed with the Atlanta Falcons—and took off! He was one of the NFL's top runners that season, scoring 17 touchdowns. He learned his lessons well!

▼ Michael Turner steps over a would-be tackler on his way to another big gain.

38

# ALL-PURPOSE BACK

Brian Westbrook of the Philadelphia Eagles is not as big as most running backs. He's just better. In 2007, he led the NFL with 2,104 **yards from scrimmage**. Along with running and catching passes, Westbrook is a standout punt returner. Westbrook has topped 1,000 rushing yards twice in his career. Without huge size but with a huge heart, he's a huge part of the Philadelphia Eagles offense.

▲ Brian Westbrook shows off his strength as he shakes off a Washington defender.

## Rookie Runners

Very few running backs become stars in their first year. In 2008, however, several did just that. Chris Johnson of the Tennessee Titans, Steve Slaton of the Houston Texans, and Matt Forte of the Chicago Bears each topped 1,200 rushing yards.

### GLOSSARY

**yards from scrimmage:** a statistic that counts up yards gained by a player running and catching passes

# Future Star: You!

**CHAPTER 5**

Running back is one of the easiest positions in football to practice. Here are some ways you and your friends can become good running backs.

## RUN LIKE A RUNNING BACK

In this drill, run so that your knees go above your waist with each step. Do this for 20 yards. Next, do 20 yards of quickstep. This means very short, quick strides. Finish with 20 yards of high-knees. Keep your shoulders and chest pointed in the direction you're running.

# QUICK STARTS

This drill combines good running starts and handoffs. Take a two- or three-point stance behind the quarterback. At "Go!" start running forward. Take a handoff and then sprint forward for 10 yards. Make sure you know which way the quarterback will turn. Practice getting a good hold of the ball.

## Warning!

Do not tackle without proper pads and adult supervision. You can easily become injured if you do not tackle in the proper way. Learn to do it right. Get help from a coach.

▶ This running back shows good form in taking the handoff from the quarterback.

# ORANGE FRIENDS

Runners need to learn to move quickly back and forth across the field. Set up cones in various spots on a field. Have a friend give you a handoff. Then dodge back and forth among the cones. Start with the cones about three yards apart. Move them closer together as you improve your "moves." This is a good way to work on your footwork and speed.

# HOLD THE BALL

A runner can't gain any yards unless he holds on to the ball. Tuck a football in your gut and hold it tightly with both hands. Run through the middle of two lines of friends as they try to pull the football out. If you don't have enough friends for this game, try it with one friend. Jog down the field, tossing a ball back and forth. Use an underhand motion. This way, you both practice receiving pitches from a quarterback.

# RECEIVING TIPS

As you read, runners have to catch, too. Catching while you're standing still is easy, though. Practice catching the ball on the run. This will let you gain more yards after you catch the ball. Stand about 10 yards to one side of your friend. When he tells you to go, run down the field a few steps. Then cut in front of your friend. (Your path will look like an L.) Have him throw the ball ahead of you, so you catch it without stopping.

## Wrapping It Up

Running backs have many jobs on a football field. They gain yards, score touchdowns, and win games. Watch running backs in action—in person or on TV—and one day you might join them!

# Record Book

Who's the best of the best? Here are the top five performers in some key rushing categories.

**Rushing Yards, Career**
1. Emmitt Smith: 18,355
2. Walter Payton: 16,726
3. Barry Sanders: 15,269
4. Curtis Martin: 14,101
5. Jerome Bettis: 13,662

**Rushing Yards, Season**
1. Eric Dickerson: 2,105 (1984)
2. Jamal Lewis: 2,066 (2003)
3. Barry Sanders: 2,053 (1997)
4. Terrell Davis: 2,008 (1998)
5. O.J. Simpson: 2,003 (1973)

**Rushing Yards, Game**
1. Adrian Peterson: 296 (2007)
2. Jamal Lewis: 295 (2006)
3. Corey Dillon: 278 (2000)
4. Walter Payton: 275 (1977)
5. O.J. Simpson: 273 (1973)

► Eric Dickerson was almost as well-known for his goggles as for his great running style.

* All records are through the 2008 season.

### Rushing Touchdowns, Career
1. Emmitt Smith: 164
2. LaDainian Tomlinson: 126
3. Marcus Allen: 123
4. Walter Payton: 115
5. Jim Brown: 106

### Rushing Touchdowns, Season
1. LaDainian Tomlinson: 28 (2006)
2. Shaun Alexander: 27 (2005)
3. Priest Holmes: 27 (2003)
4. Emmitt Smith: 25 (1995)
5. John Riggins: 24 (1983)

### Rushing Touchdowns, Game
1. Ernie Nevers: 6 (1929)
2. Jimmy Conzelman: 5 (1922)
   Jim Brown: 5 (1959)
   Cookie Gilchrist: 5 (1963)
   James Stewart: 5 (1997)
   Clinton Portis: 5 (2003)

► Emmitt Smith was not the biggest guy on the field, but he was often the best.

# Glossary

**banned:** made illegal

**defensive back:** a defensive player who is usually assigned to cover a receiver

**extra points:** kicks, worth one point, that are attempted after a touchdown is scored

**flat:** the areas to each side of the line of scrimmage, about 6 to 10 yards downfield

**formations:** the ways that football teams line up their players on the field

**hole:** an open area created by blockers into which a ball carrier can run

**huddle:** the gathering of a team's players before each play

**line of scrimmage:** the imaginary line that divides the offense and the defense before each play

**open field:** open space on the football field where runners have a lot of room to run

**option:** a play in which a running back has the choice of running with the ball or throwing it

**pitch:** a short, underhanded toss backward

**Pro Bowl:** the NFL's annual all-star game

**reverse:** a running play that starts in one direction but quickly changes to the opposite direction. It often involves a running back handing off to a receiver.

**rookie:** a player in his first season of pro football

**yards from scrimmage:** a statistic that counts up yards gained by a player running and catching passes

# Find Out More

## Books

Buckley, James. Jr. *Eyewitness Football*. New York: DK Publishing, 1999.

Gigliotti, Jim. *LaDainian Tomlinson*. Mankato, MN: Child's World, 2006.

Polzer, Tim. *Play Football!* New York: DK Publishing, 2003.

Stewart, Mark. *The Ultimate 10: Football*. Pleasantville, N.Y.: Gareth Stevens, 2009.

## Web Sites

*www.nfl.com*

The official web site of the National Football League is packed with stats, video, news, and player biographies. Football fans will find all they need about their favorite players and teams here.

*www.nflrush.com*

It's the official kids' site of the NFL. Meet star players, see video of great plays, and get tips from the pros!

# Index

# About the Author

K.C. Kelley has written nearly two dozen books on sports for young readers. He has written about football, baseball, soccer, and NASCAR. He is a former editor with the NFL and *Sports Illustrated*.